God's Love
Alive
in You

KAY ARTHUR
DAVID LAWSON

HARVEST HOUSE PUBLISHERS

EUGENE, OREGON

Cover by Koechel Peterson & Associates, Inc., Minneapolis, Minnesota

The New Inductive Study Series
GOD'S LOVE ALIVE IN YOU
Copyright © 2005 by Precept Ministries International
Published by Harvest House Publishers
Eugene, Oregon 97402
www.harvesthousepublishers.com

Library of Congress Cataloging-in-Publication Data
Arthur, Kay, 1933–
  God's love alive in you / Kay Arthur and David Lawson.
    p. cm. — (New inductive study series)
  ISBN 0-7369-1270-3 (pbk.)
  1. Bible. N.T. Epistles of John—Study and teaching. 2. Bible. N.T. Philemon—Study and teaching. 3. Bible. N.T. James—Study and teaching. I. Lawson, David. II. Title.
  BS2805.55.A78 2005
  227'.9'0071—dc22   2005000830

Printed in the United States of America

05 06 07 08 09 10 11 12 / BP-CF / 10 9 8 7 6 5 4 3 2 1

CONTENTS

ꙮꙮꙮꙮ

JAMES

ℋOW TO ℊET ꜱTARTED...

FIRST

As you study the epistles of John and James, and Paul's epistle to Philemon, you will need four things in addition to this book:

1. A Bible that you are willing to mark in. Marking is essential because it is an integral part of the learning process and will help you remember and retain what you learn. An ideal Bible for this purpose is *The New Inductive Study Bible (NISB)*. The *NISB*, available in the New American Standard Version, comes in a single-column text format with larger, easy-to-read type, and is ideal for marking. The page margins are wide and blank for note-taking.

The *NISB* is unique among all study Bibles in that it has instructions for studying each book of the Bible, but it does not contain any commentary on the text. The *NISB* isn't compiled from any particular theological stance because its purpose is to teach you how to discern truth for yourself through the inductive method of study. *Inductive* Bible study simply means that the Bible itself is the primary source for study. (The various charts that you will find in this study guide are taken from the *NISB*.) Whatever Bible you use, just know you will need to mark in it, which brings us to the second item you will need.

2. A fine-point, four-color ballpoint pen or various colored fine-point pens (such as Micron pens) for writing in

your Bible. The Micron pens are best for this purpose. Office supply stores should have these.

3. Colored pencils or an eight-color Pentel pencil.

4. A composition notebook or loose-leaf notebook for working on your assignments and recording your insights.

SECOND

1. As you study this book, you'll find specific instructions for each day's study. The study should take you between 15 and 20 minutes a day. However, just know that the more time you can give to this study, the greater the spiritual dividends and the greater your intimacy with the Word of God and the God of the Word. If you are doing this study within the framework of a class and you find the lessons too heavy, simply do what you can. To do a little is better than to do nothing. Don't be an all-or-nothing person when it comes to Bible study.

As a word of warning, you need to be aware that any time you get into the Word of God, you enter into more intensive warfare with the devil (our enemy). Why? Every piece of the Christian's armor is related to the Word of God. And the enemy doesn't want you prepared for battle. Thus, the warfare! Remember that our one and only offensive weapon is the sword of the Spirit, which is the Word of God, and it is enough to fell the enemy.

To study or not to study is a matter of choice first, discipline second. It's a matter of the heart. On what or whom are you setting your heart? Get armed for war! And remember, victory is certain.

2. As you read each chapter, train yourself to think through the content of the text by asking the "5 W's and an H": who, what, when, where, why, and how. Posing questions like these and searching out the answers help you see

exactly what the Word of God is saying. When you interrogate the text with the 5 W's and an H, you ask questions like these:

  a. **Who** are the main characters?

  b. **What** is the chapter about?

  c. **When** does this event or teaching take place?

  d. **Where** does this occur?

  e. **Why** is this being done or said?

  f. **How** did this happen?

3. The "when" of events or teachings is very important and should be marked in an easily recognizable way in your Bible. We do this by putting a clock (like the one shown here) 🕐 in the margin of our Bibles beside the verse where the time phrase occurs. Or you may want to underline references to time in one specific color. As a reminder, note on your key-word bookmark (which is explained next in this section) how you are going to mark time references in each chapter.

4. You will be told about certain key words that you should mark throughout this study. This is the purpose of the colored pencils and the colored pen. While this may seem a little time-consuming, you will discover that it is a valuable learning tool. If you will develop the habit of marking your Bible, you will find it will make a significant difference in the effectiveness of your study and in how much you retain as a result of your study.

A **key word** is an important word that is used by the author repeatedly in order to convey his message to his reader. Certain key words will show up throughout the book, while other key words will be concentrated in specific chapters or segments of the book. When you mark a key word, you should also mark its synonyms (words that have the same meaning in a particular context) and any pronouns *(he, his, she, her, it, we, they, us, our, you, their, them)* in the same way you have marked the key word. Because some people have requested them, we will give you various ideas and suggestions in your daily assignments for how you can mark different key words.

Marking words for easy identification can be done by colors, symbols, or a combination of colors and symbols. However, colors are easier to distinguish than symbols. If you use symbols, we suggest you keep them very simple. For example, one of the key words in 1 John is *love*. You could draw a red heart like this over love. If a symbol is used in marking a key word, it is best for the symbol to somehow convey the meaning of the word.

As you begin this new venture, we recommend that you devise a color-coding system for marking key words that you decide to mark throughout your Bible. Then, when you glance at the pages of your Bible, you will have instant recognition of the words.

In marking the members of the Godhead (which we do not always mark), we use a triangle to represent the **Father.** We then color it yellow. Then, playing off the triangle, we mark the Son this way: Jesus , and the Holy Spirit this way: Spirit . We find that when you mark every reference to God and Jesus, your Bible becomes cluttered. However, since the Spirit is mentioned less and because many people do not have a thorough biblical understanding of the Holy Spirit, it is good to mark all the references to the Spirit of God.

When you start marking key words, it is easy to forget how you are marking them. Therefore, we recommend that you tear out the perforated card in the back of this book and write the key words and their symbols on it. Mark the words in the way you plan to mark each in the Bible text, and then use the card as a bookmark. Make one bookmark for words you are marking throughout your Bible, and a different one for any specific book of the Bible you are studying. Or record your marking system for the words you plan to mark throughout your Bible on a blank page in your Bible.

5. AT A GLANCE charts are located at the end of each section. When you complete your study of each chapter of these books, record the main theme of that chapter on the appropriate chart. A chapter theme is a brief description or summary of the main theme or predominant subject, teaching, or event covered in that chapter.

When stating chapter themes, it is best to use words found within the text itself and to be as brief as possible. Make sure that you do them in such a way as to distinguish one chapter from another. Doing this will help you to remember what each chapter is about. In addition, it will provide you with a ready reference if you desire to find something in the book rather quickly and without a lot of page-turning.

If you develop the habit of filling out the AT A GLANCE charts as you progress through the study, you will have a complete synopsis of the book when you finish. If you have a New Inductive Study Bible, you will find the same charts in your Bible. If you record your chapter themes on the charts in your Bible and on the designated line at the head of each chapter in the text, you'll always have a quick synopsis of the chapter and the book.

6. Begin your study with prayer. Don't start without it. Why? Well, although you are doing your part to handle the Word of God accurately, remember that the Bible is a divinely inspired book. The words you are reading are absolute truth, given to you by God so that you can know Him and His ways more intimately. These truths are divinely understood.

> For to us God revealed them through the Spirit; for the Spirit searches all things, even the depths of God. For who among men knows the thoughts of a man except the spirit of the man which is in him? Even so the thoughts of God no one knows except the Spirit of God (1 Corinthians 2:10-11).

This is why you need to pray. Simply tell God you want to understand His Word so you can live accordingly. Nothing pleases Him more than obedience—honoring Him as God—as you are about to see.

7. Each day, when you finish your lesson, take some time to think about what you read, what you saw with your own eyes. Ask your heavenly Father how you can apply these insights, principles, precepts, and commands to your own life. At times, depending on how God speaks to you through His Word, you might want to record these "Lessons for Life" in the margin of your Bible next to the text you have studied. Simply put "LFL" in the margin of your Bible, then, as briefly as possible, record the lesson for life that you want to remember. You can also make the note "LFL" on your key word bookmark as a reminder to look for these when you study. You will find them encouraging (and sometimes convicting) when you come across them again. They will be a reminder of what God has shown you from His Word.

THIRD

This study is designed so that you have an assignment for every day of the week. This puts you where you should be—in the Word of God on a daily basis, grasping, systematizing, and utilizing truth. It's revolutionary!

If you will do your study daily, you will find it more profitable than doing a week's study in one sitting. Pacing yourself this way allows time for thinking through what you learn on a daily basis. However, whatever it takes to get it done, do it!

The seventh day of each week has several features that differ from the other six days. These features are designed to aid in one-on-one discipleship, group discussions, and Sunday school classes. However, they are also profitable even if you are studying this book by yourself.

The "seventh" day is whatever day in the week you choose to think about and/or discuss your week's study. On this day, you will find a verse or two to memorize and thus Store in Your Heart. This will help you focus on a major truth or truths covered in your study that week.

To assist those using the material for discipleship, family devotions, or in a Sunday school class or a group Bible study, there are Questions for Discussion or Individual Study. Whatever your situation, seeking to answer these questions will help you reason through some key issues in the study.

If you are using the study in a group setting, make sure the answers given are supported from the Bible text itself. This practice will help ensure that you are handling the Word of God accurately. As you learn to see what the text says, you will find that the Bible explains itself.

Always examine your insights by carefully observing the text to see what it *says*. Then, before you decide what the passage of Scripture *means*, make sure you interpret it in the light of its context. Context is what goes with the text...the Scriptures preceding and following what is written. Scripture will never contradict Scripture. If a Scripture passage ever seems to contradict the rest of the Word of God, you can be certain that something is being taken out of context. If you come to a passage that is difficult to understand, reserve your interpretations for a time when you can study the passage in greater depth.

Your discussion time should cause you to see how to apply these truths to your own life. What are you now going to embrace as truth? How are you going to order your life? Are you going to not only know these truths but also live accordingly?

The purpose of a THOUGHT FOR THE WEEK is to help you apply what you've learned. We've done this for your edification. In this, a little of our theology will inevitably come to the surface; however, we don't ask that you always agree with us. Rather, think through what is said in light of the context of the Word of God. You can determine how valuable it is.

Remember, books in the New Inductive Study Series are survey courses. If you want to do a more in-depth study of a particular book of the Bible, we suggest you do a Precept Upon Precept Bible Study Course on that book. The Precept studies are awesome but require five hours of personal study a week.

*I*NTRODUCTION

Jesus said, "A new commandment I give to you, that you love one another, even as I have loved you, that you also love one another. By this all men will know that you are My disciples, if you have love for one another" (John 13:34-35).

The world will know that we are Christians (disciples of Christ) by our love for one another. Have you ever thought, *That's easy for Jesus to say. He doesn't know the people I have to put up with!* You probably wouldn't say this out loud, but do you ever think it? A frustrated minister once said, "The Christian life would be easy if it weren't for the people I have to put up with." It seems that our greatest struggles involve relationships with others. Do you ever ask yourself, *How can I love the people around me? The people I work with? The people I go to church with? The people I live with? How can I love them when I have a hard enough time just tolerating them?*

Our relationships bring us not only our greatest struggles, but also our greatest joys. Relationships are important. They were at the top of Jesus' priority list. Jesus said the two most important commandments are to love God with all your heart and to love your neighbor as yourself (Matthew 22:37-40). Love is expressed in relationships, and yet relationships give us the most trouble. How well do you relate to others? How can you consistently show love not only to people you like but also to people you don't care to be around?

The Word of God has practical answers for the day-to-day struggles in our relationships.

For the next 13 weeks we will look at letters written by James, Paul, and John. From them we will gain solid, practical advice on how to love one another the way Jesus loved us so that the world will know we are His followers.

1 JOHN

INTRODUCTION TO 1 JOHN

Our world is made up of relationships. Most of us discover this truth at some point in our journey, although we all know some poor unfortunate soul who never seemed to comprehend the idea.

In this life, we all have two types of relationships. The first and most important is a vertical one—your relationship with God. This one is serious. Your relationship with God determines everything else in this life and in the life to come. The second is horizontal—your relationship with others. Both require time and effort. Certain skills will make both work smoother. And we can do some things to injure both.

In this first letter from John the apostle to the church, we will learn some things about horizontal and vertical relationships. We will also see how to develop some skills that will make them work smoother.

CONDITIONS FOR FELLOWSHIP

Fellowship is the fuel that drives relationships. Relationships thrive on time spent together, and without it, they tend to fall apart. This is true for both your relationship with God and your relationships with others. This week we will look at the first chapter of 1 John, and we will spend some time considering the idea of fellowship. Dedicate a page in your notebook to everything you discover about fellowship. By the end of the week you will have learned a lot about the topic.

DAY ONE

The best way to get a feel for a letter is to read it in one sitting. This helps you see the flow of thought and sometimes the author's purpose in writing.

Your assignment today is to read 1 John in one sitting. The letter has only five short chapters, so it is easily readable in a few minutes. Begin with prayer, asking God to give you an understanding of this book. As you read, mark in a distinctive way or with a distinctive color each reference to *writing* or *write*.

Now that you have finished, record (in your own words) John's purpose for writing this letter.

DAY TWO

The rest of this week we will focus our time and energy on 1 John 1. Today read chapter 1 and mark *God* and *Jesus* the way demonstrated on page 8. Make sure you include the pronouns.

When you have finished, list in your notebook what you learned by marking these words. Be sure to answer the "who, what, when, where, why, and how" questions.

Now, for your last assignment today, turn to the gospel of John and read 1:1-5,14-18. List in your notebook what these passages teach you about Jesus. If you have time after this assignment, meditate on what you have learned about the Word of Life.

DAY THREE

Your assignment is to read 1 John 1:1-10 again. This time as you read, draw an arch above the word *light,* and shade it yellow. Shade *darkness* black or gray. Draw a blue figure eight above the word *fellowship.* Make sure to include appropriate synonyms.

In your notebook, list what you learn about *light, darkness,* and *fellowship* from chapter 1.

Now, read the following passages and note what you learn about *light, darkness,* and *fellowship.*

- ∾ Matthew 5:14-16
- ∾ 2 Corinthians 6:14-15

DAY FOUR

You have already noticed the two types of fellowship in 1 John 1: fellowship with the Father and fellowship with other believers. As we said earlier, fellowship is the fuel that drives relationships. That means that if something injures the fellowship, it will injure the relationship. Well, friend, John writes about something that injures fellowship. Today we will take a closer look at what that is and how it affects the relationship.

Read chapter 1 again slowly and shade each reference to *sin* brown. Mark *truth* like this: truth. Underline the phrase *if we say* in red.

In your notebook, list what you learn about *sin* and *truth* from chapter one.

Finally, before you wrap up for today, read the following passages to see what you learn about truth, especially since it involves our relationship with God. You will see very familiar verses in each passage. Pay close attention to the contexts where the familiar verses are found.

   ∾ John 3:16-21

   ∾ John 8:31-32

DAY FIVE

Read 1 John 1. When you have finished, record the main idea of chapter 1 on 1 JOHN AT A GLANCE on page 49.

As you have noticed, we sometimes ask you to look at passages other than the primary one you are studying. This is called cross-referencing. Cross-referencing is invaluable because the best interpreter of Scripture is Scripture itself. Looking at other places in the Word where an idea is discussed will shed light on the passage you're studying.

For this reason, your second assignment is to read the following passages and record everything you learn about fellowship in your notebook.

- Acts 2:37-42 (Peter has just preached his sermon on Pentecost day.)

- 1 Corinthians 1:9

- 2 Corinthians 13:14 (KJV and NKJV use the word "communion.")

- Hebrews 13:16 ("Sharing" is a translation of the same Greek word as "fellowship." The KJV uses the word "communicate.")

DAY SIX

We will look at chapter 2 more in depth next week. For now, getting a feel for the chapter will be enough. Read chapter 2 and mark the word *abide* (and synonyms such as *lives, remained,* and *continued*) with a diamond.

In this passage, *lives, remained,* and *continued* are all translated from the same Greek word as *abide.* The NIV uses the word "lives." When you have finished, list in your notebook what you learn about abiding.

DAY SEVEN

Store in your heart: 1 John 1:6-7

Read and discuss: 1 John 1:1-10

QUESTIONS FOR DISCUSSION OR INDIVIDUAL STUDY

- What does John say his purpose is for writing this letter?

- Of all of the reasons John gives for writing, which one seems to override the others?

- Why is it important to know whether you have eternal life?

- What did you learn this week about Jesus, the Word of Life?

- What did you learn about fellowship?

- How do our actions support or deny our claims to be in fellowship with the Father?

- Whom are believers supposed to have fellowship with?

- What things injure fellowship with God? What things injure your fellowship with others?

- Have you ever injured your fellowship with others or with God? How?

- What are you personally responsible to do in order to have fellowship with God? With others?

- What did you learn this week about sin?

- What's true of someone who says he has no sin? Of someone who says he has never sinned? Of someone who admits (confesses) his sin?

- How do these truths apply to you?

- What did you learn about darkness, light, and your personal walk this week?

THOUGHT FOR THE WEEK

The first condition for fellowship with God is walking in the light. The second is dealing honestly with your sin.

The Greek word translated "fellowship" in the New Testament is *koinōnia*. The word means to share in, to participate together with. It implies the idea of having something in common. God is light, and in Him is no darkness at all. If we say we have fellowship with Him, yet we walk in darkness, we have a problem. Why? Because God is light, and light cannot have fellowship with darkness. Darkness and light have nothing in common.

Walking in darkness is synonymous with walking in sin. Sin injures the fellowship we have with God. Has God ever seemed distant to you? Have you ever felt as if your prayers were reaching only as high as the ceiling? Have you been in worship services when you simply did not feel His presence and you were maybe even a little annoyed with worshippers around you who seemed to be in touch with Him? Friend, the trouble may be that you are walking in darkness.

Fellowship with God is not the only relationship injured by sin. Your relationship with others is also damaged. What fellowship does darkness have with light? When you walk in the darkness, other believers will seem distant from you. Sin injures your walk with God, and because believers are His children (John 1:12) it also injures your walk with them. Fellowship fuels relationships. Walking in sin stops the fellowship and injures the relationship.

Where are you walking? In prayer, ask God to reveal any area of your life where you are walking in darkness. What do you do when He exposes some area of sin in your life? You go back to 1 John 1:9. He will cleanse you and place you back in the light.

Spend some time today with God. Let Him search your heart for anything that needs to be brought to the light.

Cautions to Fellowship

Fellowship with God takes priority over our fellowship with other believers. It takes priority over every other relationship in our lives. One of the reasons John wrote this letter is "so that you may know that you have eternal life" (1 John 5:13). In other words, He is laying out the requirements for fellowship with God.

Last week we explored John's first two conditions for enjoying fellowship with God and with other believers. This week we will look at other conditions for fellowship, and we will also examine some cautions to fellowship.

DAY ONE

Last week you read 1 John 2 and marked each reference to *abide* and some synonyms. Today read chapter 2 again and mark the following words along with any synonyms or pronouns: *sin, Jesus, God.*

When you have finished, add to your notebook what you learn about fellowship from 1 John 2:1-6.

DAY TWO

Read 1 John 2 again. As you read, mark each reference to *light* and *darkness* just as you did on day 3 of last week.

By the way, if you are reading from the updated version of the New American Standard Bible, "Light" is capitalized to indicate that the translators believe it refers to one of the persons of the Trinity.

When you have finished reading and marking, list in your notebook what you learn about light and darkness. Also, add new insights to your list on fellowship, especially as it relates to light and darkness.

DAY THREE

We realize that reading a chapter over and over may seem redundant at times, but we have personally experienced the value of repetition. Each time you read a chapter, you are imprinting Scripture on your mind, and you are facing the possibility of seeing some new truth you have never noticed. We are not trying to bore you; we are giving you every opportunity to see the truth of Scripture for yourself.

That said, guess what your assignment will be. Correct—read chapter 2 again. Today mark the word *love* with a heart and shade it red. Draw a heart with a slash through it over the word *hate*. Print a large K over the word *know*. Be sure to mark any synonyms. Then list new insights in your notebook. For the rest of our study in 1 John we will look at the word *know*. Start a two-column chart in your notebook of what you learn by marking the word *know*. One column will be "What I Can Know," and the other will be "How I Can Know It."

DAY FOUR

When you marked *love* yesterday, you probably noticed the first warning John gives in 2:15-17. He cautions us about things that will affect our fellowship with God and with other believers. The first part of your assignment is to read 1 John 2:15-17 and list the characteristics of the world, especially those given in verse 16.

The second part of your assignment is to read Genesis 3:1-7. List the characteristics of the fruit of the tree of the knowledge of good and evil. Compare the characteristics of the fruit with the characteristics of the world. How are these things apparent in our world today?

DAY FIVE

No doubt you have noticed John's second caution to believers in 1 John 2:18-29. False teachers or antichrists were trying to deceive believers. The same is true today; false teachers are still in the world. What defense do we have to keep us from being deceived?

To answer this question, read 2:18-29 and mark in some distinctive fashion each reference to *anointing*. When you have finished, read the following passages and list what you learn about the Holy Spirit. How are the Holy Spirit and the anointing similar?

- John 16:5-16
- 1 Corinthians 6:19-20
- James 4:5

DAY SIX

In today's society, all religions are welcome—unless they are exclusive. To say that your approach to God is the only valid approach is a social sin of the highest order. As long as one is sincere and believes in something, his or her beliefs are accepted as valid. The question is, do all roads lead to heaven? Are all beliefs true? Does it matter whom you place your trust in?

Read 1 John 2:15-29, paying close attention to verse 23. Compare what you learn to teachings in the following cross-references.

- John 8:12
- John 14:6

Can we have a relationship with God aside from Jesus Christ? Are you sure?

Add the theme of chapter 2 to your 1 JOHN AT A GLANCE chart.

DAY SEVEN

Store in your heart: 1 John 2:1-3
Read and discuss: 1 John 2:1-29

QUESTIONS FOR DISCUSSION OR INDIVIDUAL STUDY

- What did you learn this week about fellowship with God?
- What should our relationship with sin be like?
- What happens when we sin?

∾ Who is Jesus according to what you have seen this week?

∾ How do light and darkness relate to love and hate?

∾ How does this apply to you personally?

∾ Do you hate any brothers in Christ?

∾ What would hating fellow believers say about your walk?

∾ What are we commanded to not love?

∾ What practical steps can you take to avoid falling in love with this world and the things in this world?

∾ Discuss 1 John 2:15-17 and compare these verses to Genesis 3:1-7.

∾ How do you define "lust of the flesh"?

∾ What are some examples of "lust of the eyes" and "the boastful pride of life"?

∾ In what ways do you see these drives tugging at your own life?

∾ What did you learn about anointing this week?

∾ Do you have the anointing from the Holy One?

THOUGHT FOR THE WEEK

People in our society often divorce their belief system from their behavior. Sometimes it seems that almost everyone claims to have a relationship with God. At the same time, immorality, drug and alcohol use, greed, selfishness, pride, and violence dominate the entertainment industry and the evening news. These things are not consistent with godliness. Something is wrong.

This problem is not new. John addresses the same issues. "The one who says, 'I have come to know Him,' and does not keep His commandments, is a liar, and the truth is not in him" (1 John 2:4).

John makes his point with great simplicity. You can't divorce your beliefs from your behavior. If you're a Christian, it will show in your actions. Friend, how does your life look? If we were watching you, would we know you were a Christian by your lifestyle?

Another problem area in society is the pressure to be all-inclusive in matters of religion. The prevailing idea is that all religions and belief systems are equally correct and valid. In fact, the only thing that invalidates a religion is its claim to be exclusively true.

The truth is, Jesus made very exclusive claims, and so did His disciples. In 1 John 2:23, John writes, "Whoever denies the Son does not have the Father; the one who confesses the Son has the Father also." Sounds pretty exclusive, doesn't it? He's saying no one has fellowship with the Father aside from a relationship with the Son.

Two roads that contradict—that head in opposite directions—can't both lead to heaven. You saw this week that Jesus claims to be the *only* way to heaven. Think about it. Either Jesus told the truth and is the only way or else He *did not and is not.* No middle ground exists.

Where do you stand, friend? Are you trying to be all-inclusive? Have you bought the idea that Jesus is one of many ways to heaven? You saw the truth this week in the Word of God. Now you must choose. "Choose for yourselves today whom you will serve...but as for me and my house, we will serve the LORD" (Joshua 24:15).

CHARACTERISTICS OF FELLOWSHIP: RIGHTEOUSNESS

We have seen the conditions for fellowship with God and other believers: fellowship with Jesus and walking in the light. We looked at some cautions concerning fellowship with God, such as "do not love the world nor the things in the world" (1 John 2:15). This week we will study 1 John 3 and some of the conditions necessary for fellowship. You will notice some of the topics seem familiar. They are because John intends to keep reminding us that sin can destroy our fellowship with God and with other people.

DAY ONE

Read 1 John 3 today three times, marking one of the following words each time: *sin, God,* and *Jesus.*

In chapter 3, determining whether a pronoun refers to God the Father or God the Son can be very difficult. Don't let this frustrate you. Usually pronouns refer to the last mentioned noun. Do the best you can and move on. The Father, Son, and Holy Spirit are after all one God. If you mark one with the wrong symbol, it's okay.

DAY TWO

One of the goals of inductive study is to learn everything you can about God the Father, God the Son, and God the Holy Spirit. Yesterday you read 1 John 3 and marked each reference to the Father and to the Son. Today read chapter 3 once again and list everything you learn about God and Jesus in your notebook. When you have finished, read over your list and spend some time meditating on the truths you have learned.

DAY THREE

In your notebook, draw a two-column chart. One side title "Children of God," and the other side "Children of the Devil." Read chapter 3, and as you read, mark *children* (shade it blue).

When you have finished, list everything you gleaned concerning children of God and children of the devil from verses 1-10.

At first read, this passage can be a little unnerving. We all know we have sinned, even after becoming believers, yet John says no one born of God practices sin. The key to understanding this passage is the word "practice." John is talking about people who sin habitually—they practice it. As you do this assignment, watch the word "practice" and ask yourself, *What are the characteristics of fellowship with God?*

DAY FOUR

Today read 1 John 3 three times. Each time you read, mark one of the following words using the symbols or colors you used before, including any synonyms you find: *love, hate,* and *know.*

Now, no shortcuts with this assignment! We know you'll be tempted to simply read through once and mark everything, but you may miss what God has for you. Reading through three times will really help you see the flow of thought. When you have finished, add to your chart everything else you learn about the characteristics of children of God and children of the devil.

DAY FIVE

Your assignment today is short and simple. Read 1 John 3. When you have finished, first, list in your notebook everything you learn about love and hate. Second, add everything you learned by marking *know* to your "What I Can Know" chart.

And last, add the main idea or theme of chapter 3 to your 1 JOHN AT A GLANCE chart.

DAY SIX

In 1 John 3:13, John gives some wise counsel: "Do not be surprised, brethren, if the world hates you." Today we will cross-reference this idea that the world hates believers.

Read 1 John 3 one more time. When you have finished, read the following verses and learn what you can about the attitude of the world toward believers in Christ. As you read, ask the "who, what, when, where, why, and how" questions.

- ∽ John 15:18-25—Why does the world hate us? Why do they hate Jesus?

- ∽ Luke 6:20-23—Who will be blessed? How will they be blessed?

DAY SEVEN

Store in your heart: 1 John 3:18
Read and discuss: 1 John 3

QUESTIONS FOR DISCUSSION OR INDIVIDUAL STUDY

- ∽ Discuss the characteristics of God and of Jesus Christ you learned this week.

- ∽ What are the characteristics of a child of the devil?

- ∽ What are the characteristics of a child of God?

- ∽ How does the word *practice* help you understand these characteristics?

- ∽ Which family does hate belong to?

- ∽ Discuss the cross-references you did on hate and the world. Why does the world hate believers?

∽ Does the world hate you? Have you ever noticed this attitude from the world?

∽ How does your life reflect the family characteristics of a child of God?

∽ In what practical ways can you show love to the people around you?

THOUGHT FOR THE WEEK

Spiritually speaking, you are going to look like your Father. You will take on the characteristics of the one you belong to.

You saw this truth this week in 1 John 3. The key to understanding this passage is the word *practice* (NASB and the English Standard Version). John is not saying a child of God never sins. He made that point in 1 John 1:8: "If we say that we have no sin, we are deceiving ourselves." John's point is that our lifestyle is what counts. Are you practicing sin—not an occasional mishap but as the habit of your life?

Friend, if you are, you need to stop and examine your life. No one who is born of God practices sin, according to God's Word. As a matter of fact, John shows us two easy ways to recognize believers: Do they practice righteousness? Do they love their brother? How about you—whom do you look like?

Fellowship with other believers depends on you loving them. Love and time are closely related. Loving someone is difficult if you never spend any time with them.

To love is to meet needs. Jesus gave us the perfect example of this when He laid down His life for us (1 John 3:16). It takes time to learn enough about someone to know their hurts, their pains, their joys. Loving your neighbor starts with taking the time to get to know your neighbor. In our fast-paced society, time is our most important commodity.

We challenge you to plan to spend some of your most precious resource getting to know someone who needs to be loved. Who might that be? Pray, asking God to bring someone across your path. Then begin to build a relationship and learn enough about this person to be able to pray specifically for him or her.

CHARACTERISTICS OF FELLOWSHIP: LOVE

There is a song from the '70s titled "Love Will Keep Us Together." The idea is true for the church. Love will keep us together.

DAY ONE

Read 1 John 4. The key to Bible study is to read the Bible. We know this sounds simple, but too many times Christians reach for a book *about* the Bible when they could open the Word itself instead. That said, your assignment is to read chapter 4 twice, marking each reference to the following words, including synonyms and pronouns: *know, God, Jesus Christ, Holy Spirit.*

DAY TWO

Read 1 John 4 again. Don't mark anything today—just read. But may we suggest you read aloud? Many students find that reading a passage out loud helps them remember the passage better.

When you have finished reading, add everything you learn about God, Jesus Christ, and the Holy Spirit to your lists. Then add what you learned by marking the word *know* to your "What I Can Know" chart.

DAY THREE

As you have read 1 John, you have probably noticed that one of John's favorite ways of addressing his readers is "beloved." It is a term of endearment; literally, it means dearly loved one. As you read chapter 4 today, underline *beloved.* This exercise will help you identify the commands John gives us in this chapter. When you have finished reading, make a list of the instructions or commands you find in this chapter.

DAY FOUR

Read 1 John 4 and mark each occurrence of the word *love* just as you have been doing. Then list what you learn about love from this passage.

Add the theme of 1 John 4 to 1 JOHN AT A GLANCE.

DAY FIVE

You have already seen that the Word of God defines the true believer as one who loves his brother—a very serious matter. Today look up these cross-references and see what you can learn about love. Record your insights by asking the "who, what, when, where, why, and how" questions.

- ∾ Matthew 5:43-48
- ∾ Mark 12:28-34
- ∾ John 13:34-35
- ∾ Romans 13:8-10
- ∾ James 2:8-17

DAY SIX

Today you will continue studying cross-references to see what the Bible says about the subject of love and how we are to treat others. Add your insights to your notebook.

- ∾ 1 Corinthians 16:13-14
- ∾ Galatians 5:13-24
- ∾ Colossians 3:12-17

DAY SEVEN

 Store in your heart: 1 John 4:15-16
Read and discuss: 1 John 4

QUESTIONS FOR DISCUSSION OR INDIVIDUAL STUDY

- ∾ According to 1 John 4, how can we identify the Spirit of God as opposed to the spirit of the antichrist? Practically speaking, what does this involve?

∽ What has God shown you this week about Himself?

∽ Discuss what you learned about Jesus from 1 John 4.

∽ In what ways has God shown His love for us?

∽ Taking in to consideration everything you learned this week, what are some of the characteristics of the child of God?

∽ In what ways can you show love to people you come in contact with?
  • Your neighbors?
  • Your family?
  • Someone who has offended you?
  • Someone who has injured you?

∽ Has God given you the opportunity to love someone this week? How did you do?

Thought for the Week

A few years ago a private Christian group put together an ad campaign called "God Speaks." They placed sayings "from God" on billboards all around the U.S. One of them read,

> That "Love thy neighbor" thing...I meant it.
> God

You got that impression this week, didn't you? God really does take loving your neighbor seriously. We are called to love our brothers, our families, our neighbors, and even our enemies. In fact, this is the dividing line between the world and us. It's by our love the world will know that we are disciples of Christ.

Unfortunately, organized religion has not always shown that kind of love. You'll remember the Pharisees were always angry when Jesus healed someone on the Sabbath instead of being happy that someone was healed. Some churches seem to be known by their divisions and just plain meanness rather than by love. Our doctrine is skewed if we are going to church on Sunday, wearing the right clothes, and hanging around pretty buildings in order to be identified as disciples of Christ. Our love for one another is what sets us apart. And not just our love for one another but also our love for our enemies. Jesus said loving only the people that love you doesn't impress anyone. Now, loving your enemy—that would be impressive. Why? The world doesn't do it.

How are you doing? Are you showing love to people God brings across your path? Is your attitude one of gentleness and caring? Or would meanness and contrariness better describe you? Ask God to give you a spiritual checkup.

CONSEQUENCES OF
FELLOWSHIP: WE WIN!

ᕲᕲᕲᕲ

We win! We win! We win because whoever is "born of God overcomes the world" (1 John 5:4). Do you feel like a winner? Or do you sometimes feel as if you're losing? Friend, we win! In this last week of our study of 1 John, we will learn about overcoming.

DAY ONE

Today your assignment is to read 1 John 5. Two passages in this chapter are hard to understand (verses 6-8 and verse 16), and not everyone agrees on what they mean. Don't let this slow you down. Stay focused on the task at hand, and we will take a closer look at these passages later this week. As you read, mark each reference to *God, Jesus,* and *Holy Spirit,* including pronouns.

When you have finished, add what you learn about the Godhead from verses 1-12 to your list. There is no need to go further; this is enough for today.

DAY TWO

Read chapter 5. As you read, circle the word *world*. Read slowly and aloud; you have plenty of time. Then finish your list on God's nature by recording what you learn in verses 13-21.

DAY THREE

Read 1 John 5. As you read, mark each reference to *sin* and *know*.

When you have finished, list everything you learned by marking *sin*. Then, complete your "What I Can Know" chart. This is your final day to work on this chart. After you are finished, take some time to review and meditate on what the Lord has shown you.

DAY FOUR

Are we overcomers? Read 1 John 5:1-5 and underline each reference to *overcomes*. When you have finished, list what you learned by asking the "5 W's and an H" questions. The Greek word for "overcomes" in verse 4 is in the present tense. This specifies a continuous action as opposed to a one-time event. It carries the idea of a pattern or habit of life. Now reread this passage with this brief explanation in mind.

Read the following verses and see what insights they add to your understanding.

- ∞ John 16:29-33
- ∞ Romans 12:21
- ∞ 1 John 2:13-14

Who overcomes?

DAY FIVE

Read 1 John 5 and use a T to mark references to *testimony* or *testifies*.

Now read the following cross-references and compare them to 1 John 5:6-12.

- ∞ Matthew 3:13-17
- ∞ John 19:33-37

DAY SIX

As a rule, the best way to approach a passage of Scripture is to keep it simple. You want to let the text speak for itself, not to burden it with your presuppositions. With this idea of simplicity in mind, read 1 John 5. Now let's think through verses 16-18 with the following questions:

- ∞ Who should we pray for according to verse 16?
- ∞ What does the description "brother" imply about the person?
- ∞ What is the occasion for the prayer?

 ∾ Does John forbid prayer for a brother committing
    a sin leading to death, or does he simply not com-
    mand prayer for him?

 ∾ What two sins are discussed in this passage?

We realize this exercise will not answer all your questions about "a sin leading to death," but you have walked
through this passage in a logical fashion and gleaned all of
the facts John gives us. The first step to understanding any
passage is to know for certain what it says. You now know
exactly what it says.

Add the theme of chapter 5 to 1 JOHN AT A GLANCE
and then add the theme of the entire book.

DAY SEVEN

 Store in your heart: 1 John 5:2-3
    Read and discuss: 1 John 5

QUESTIONS FOR DISCUSSION OR INDIVIDUAL STUDY

 ∾ What did you learn about God this week?

 ∾ Discuss what you learned about Jesus this week.

 ∾ According to 1 John 5, *what* can you know and *how?*

 ∾ What did you learn about overcoming the world? Who
    overcomes? How? When?

 ∾ When the text says Jesus came by "water and blood,"
    what do these refer to?

 ∾ What is the testimony of God?

ᖇ Why has John written these things?

ᖇ Can you *know* you have eternal life? How do you know you have eternal life?

ᖇ How should we respond when we see a brother or sister committing a sin?

ᖇ Are we forbidden to pray in certain cases?

ᖇ What have you learned in this study of 1 John that will make a difference in your relationship with God? In your relationship with others?

Thought for the Week

Jesus said, "In the world you will have tribulation, but take courage; I have overcome the world" (John 16:33). Take courage; He has overcome the world.

Do you need to hear that this week? If not this week, then hear it anyway because you'll need it at some point. In this world, we all have tribulation. It comes in different ways and at different times, but tribulation and trouble always come. The word *tribulation* means to press down, to pressure, to crush. Do you ever feel crushed by the world, by circumstances, by life itself? Do you ever wonder if you can take the pressure? Take courage, friend; Jesus has overcome the world, and because He won, we win.

So the war is already won, but how do you handle the battles? John gives us the key in verses 14-15: you ask God anything according to His will. You go to your heavenly Father in prayer and you go in confidence. Bring your troubles to the throne room of heaven and talk to God about them. This may sound simplistic, but it works. As we pray, God strengthens us with His peace. As we pray, God assures our spirit that He understands and that He is watching us. As we pray, our hearts are reassured. As we pray, He reminds us that we win. Who overcomes? We do!

By the way, the word "overcomes" in 1 John 5:4 is a translation of the Greek word *nikao*, meaning "I conquer." Its associate noun, *nike*, means "victory" (from which we get the name of the famous brand of sportswear). We win because Jesus has the victory!

Theme of 1 John:

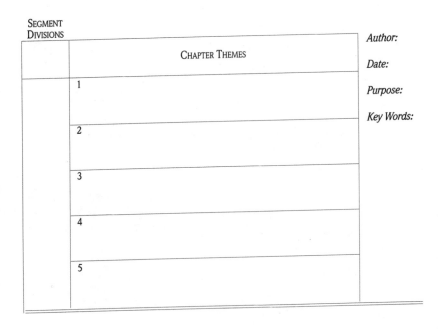

SEGMENT
DIVISIONS

CHAPTER THEMES

1

2

3

4

5

Author:

Date:

Purpose:

Key Words:

2 JOHN

WALK
IN LOVE

John and his brother James met Jesus through the preaching of John the Baptist. According to Matthew 4:21-22 they left the family fishing business to follow Him.

Early on, Jesus referred to them as the "Sons of Thunder." But something happened to change John because in his writings, love is one of the dominant themes. The former Son of Thunder was humbled to the point that, aside from the book of Revelation, he doesn't even mention himself by name in his own writings.

Although John doesn't identify himself directly, the early church fathers were unanimous in identifying him as the author of 1, 2, and 3 John, Revelation, and the Gospel of John. This second letter from John is one of the shortest books in the Bible, but it has a clear relevance to our situation today.

DAY ONE

As always, begin your time in prayer. Specifically ask God to show you what He has for you to learn from this book. You will be asked to read through 2 John at least once each day. Please do not miss this opportunity. Reading the Word of God repeatedly can be very valuable. John has woven together a connection of thoughts in this letter to support one cohesive point. By reading it each day you will begin to see the flow of thought and John's point, not just the individual verses. In addition to this, if you will read it slowly and out loud each day, you will find that by the end of the week you almost have it memorized.

Today start by reading through this short little book in its entirety without marking anything. Read it as if it were a letter written just to you.

Now read through 2 John again. Mark every reference (including pronouns) to the author (draw a blue circle around it) and to the recipients (draw a red square around it).

When you have finished, list in your notebook what you learn about the author and the recipients of the letter. Pay close attention to the relationship between them.

Who is the chosen lady?

DAY TWO

Yesterday you looked at the author and the recipients of this letter. Who is the chosen lady? A church? An individual? Scholars are divided in their opinions, but many people through the ages have believed John was writing to a local church congregation, which he calls the "chosen lady." If this is true, then the lady's children would be the members of the congregation—believers. How are these children supposed to be walking? The answer has implications for us as children of God.

Read 2 John slowly and out loud. Mark each reference to *love* with a heart just as you have before. Don't forget the synonyms. Read the letter through again and mark *walking* with a set of legs like this: **walking.**

When you have finished, list in your notebook what you learn by marking these words.

Finally, read the following passages to see what additional insights you can gain concerning *love* and how we are to act or walk.

- ∾ Leviticus 19:18
- ∾ Deuteronomy 6:4-9

So, how is your walk?

DAY THREE

Today read 2 John (you are not really surprised, are you?) and mark *abide* with a diamond. Mark *truth* like this: truth.

When you have finished, list what you have learned by marking *abide* and *truth*.

Finally, read the following passages to see what additional insights they give on truth, abiding, and our walk as children of God.

- ∾ 1 John 2:6,14; 3:24; 4:13-16 (These are review.)
- ∾ John 8:31-32; 15:3-10

Are you abiding in the truth?

DAY FOUR

Start by reading 2 John at least once. When you have finished, read the following passages and mark the word *love* with a heart and shade it red. Pay careful attention to *whom* we are to love.

- ∾ Matthew 5:43-48 (This is review from your 1 John study.)
- ∾ Mark 12:28-34
- ∾ John 15:1-17

DAY FIVE

Why did John write this letter? In 1 John he stated plainly his reason for writing, but what about this second letter? Why the emphasis on walking in love?

You have noticed by now that John contrasts the actions of believers with another group mentioned in this letter. Today read 2 John and underline each reference to *deceivers*.

When you have finished, list in your notebook all that you learn about *deceivers* from 2 John.

By the way, the word "for" in verse 7 is a translation of the Greek word *hoti*, which is also frequently translated "because." As your last assignment today, reread 2 John, inserting the word *because* in place of *for* in verse 7. What is John explaining in verse 7 by saying *for* or *because*? What are the characteristics of the deceivers? Does this truth apply to us today?

DAY SIX

This is your last day in 2 John. Our prayer is that the Lord has driven home His point concerning love, truth, and our relationship with others.

One of the characteristics of deceivers is that they deny Jesus came in the flesh. Some have taught that Jesus did not really come to earth in flesh and blood. They say His spirit was here, but He was never flesh and blood. What does the Word say? Read John 1:1-17 and mark each reference to the *word*. Then reread 1 John 4:1-3. Has Jesus come in the flesh?

When you have finished, read 2 John and then fill in the 2 JOHN AT A GLANCE chart located on page 60.

You will notice that this chart is a little different from the James and 1 John charts. There are no chapter breaks in this letter. This chart is divided by paragraphs. In your Bible the paragraphs may be designated in several different ways depending on which version and type you are using. Some Bibles use a break in the text, and some will even indent the verse number. The New American Standard Bible uses bold verse numbers to indicate paragraph divisions.

DAY SEVEN

Store in your heart: 2 John 6

Read and discuss: 2 John

QUESTIONS FOR DISCUSSION OR INDIVIDUAL STUDY

∞ According to the passages you read this week, whom are you to love?

∞ Who is the "one another" you are supposed to love according to John 15:1-17?

~ What are some practical ways you can show love to one another?

~ Who is the neighbor you are called to love according to Mark 12:28-34?

~ What are some practical ways you can show love to your "neighbor"?

~ Who are your enemies? How can you show them love?

~ How will this week's study change the way you respond to people?

~ What did you learn about abiding in the truth this week?

~ Discuss the characteristics of the deceivers. How are they described? What sets them apart?

~ Contrast the deceivers with the believers.

~ Did Jesus come in flesh and blood to the earth? What difference would it make if He did not?

~ What has God taught you personally this week?

THOUGHT FOR THE WEEK

One of the great differences between believers and the ones John refers to as "deceivers" or "antichrists" is the presence of love in the believer's life. As Christians we are commanded to love one another. This is the sign that shows the world we belong to Christ.

> A new commandment I give to you, that you love one another, even as I have loved you, that you also love one another. By this all men

will know that you are My disciples, if you
have love for one another (John 13:34-35).

The gravity of this statement is overwhelming. The
world will be able to tell we are Christians because of our
love for each other. So, how is your advertising campaign
going? Are you advertising that you belong to Jesus?

We are also told to love our neighbor. This is more than
simply being careful where you live so you will always have
neighbors who are easy to love. When the Jews asked Jesus
who their neighbor was, He told them the story of the good
Samaritan. The Samaritan helped an injured Jew by providing first aid and paying for his lodging until he was well
enough to travel. The key to the story is that the Jews and
Samaritans hated each other. The hero in this story loved
someone who probably would have hated him.

Are you loving the people around you? Do you ever go
out of your way to help the people who don't love you? Do
you actively seek ways to love your neighbor?

The last category is loving your enemy. Jesus was very
clear about this. Love your enemy. Do good to those who
persecute you. How are you doing? Have you found ways to
love your enemy?

Remember, the deceivers are characterized not only by
wrong beliefs but also wrong actions. They don't walk in
love.

The key to relationships is to love one another.

Theme of 2 John:

	SEGMENT DIVISIONS	PARAGRAPH THEMES
Author:		
Date:		VERSES 1-3
Purpose:		VERSES 4-6
Key Words:		VERSES 7-11
		VERSE 12
		VERSE 13

3 JOHN

LOVE WALKS IN TRUTH

Love cares about the individual. Love encourages. Love rebukes. Love walks in truth. And so, in love, John wrote a third epistle before he was exiled to Patmos. Love is the key to developing relationships; therefore, we need to study this letter.

DAY ONE

As always, begin with prayer.

As we did last week, we will ask you to read through this letter at least once each day. Our prayer is that you did this as you studied 2 John and have already seen the benefit of saturating your mind with Scripture. Your first two days will be spent becoming familiar with this letter.

Your assignment is to read through this short little book in its entirety without stopping to mark anything.

Read through it again and mark every reference (including pronouns) to the author (circle it in blue) and the recipient (box it in red).

In your notebook, list what you learn about them, especially what you learn about their relationship with each other. Enough for today; close your time in prayer.

DAY TWO

Begin your study with prayer. Afterward, read 3 John once through without stopping to mark any words. Now, read 3 John a second time. This time mark each occurrence of the word *love* with a heart and shade it red, and mark *truth* like this: truth.

After you have finished, record what you have learned about love and truth. Ask yourself, how does John use the word *truth*? In other words, how does John define truth?

DAY THREE

Read 3 John. Read it again, this time underlining each reference to the *brethren* (*brothers* in the NIV and English Standard Version) first mentioned in verse 5. Be sure to catch all of the pronouns John uses.

When you have finished, list in your notebook what you learn about these men. Answer as many of the five W's and an H questions as you can. Be sure to take note of who supports them, who doesn't, and how.

DAY FOUR

In our society today, hospitality is essentially a lost art. We tend to look at hospitality as too time-consuming and too inconvenient for us to bother with. However, hospitality in the ancient world was extremely important. Hotels in the ancient world were costly and had an evil reputation. Traveling Christians, such as missionaries or itinerant preachers, were dependent on the hospitality of other believers. In this letter we see that two church leaders—Gaius and Diotrephes—had differing views on the issue of hospitality. For the next two days we will look at this subject and see what the rest of Scripture has to say about showing kindness to others.

First, let's look at the required attitude for church leaders. Start by reading 3 John once through to establish the context in your mind. Then read the following passages and in your notebook list what you learn about hospitality. We will look at a few more passages tomorrow.

- ∾ Romans 12:10-13
- ∾ 1 Timothy 3:1-3 (*Overseer* is synonymous with *elder* and describes a position of leadership within the church.)
- ∾ Titus 1:7-9

DAY FIVE

The Greek word translated "hospitality" in the passages you studied yesterday is *philoxenia* which literally translated is "to love strangers." So the idea is that to be hospitable is to treat strangers as if they were friends and brothers.

Today read 3 John again. Then read the following passages and add what you learn about hospitality to your list from day four.

- ❧ Matthew 25:35-40—(The word *hospitality* is not used in this passage, but these verses provide a great example of how we are to be hospitable.)
- ❧ Hebrews 13:1-3
- ❧ 1 Peter 4:8-9

DAY SIX

This is your last day in 3 John. We pray it has opened your eyes to how serious God is about showing kindness to others.

Start by reading 3 John and mark the word *good* by coloring it green.

When you have finished, list in your notebook everything you learn about John's use of the word *good*.

Before you go, be sure to fill in your 3 JOHN AT A GLANCE chart found on page 69. You will notice the chart is divided into paragraphs just like 2 JOHN AT A GLANCE.

DAY SEVEN

Store in your heart: 3 John 11
Read and discuss: 3 John

QUESTIONS FOR DISCUSSION OR INDIVIDUAL STUDY

- ❧ What is John's reason for writing this letter? Or what was the motivating cause behind this letter?

∾ What did you learn about the truth this week?

∾ Compare John's definition of *truth* to the way we use the word today.

∾ What did you learn about love this week?

∾ How does John say we are to treat the brethren?

∾ What did you learn this week about being hospitable?

∾ How are you supporting those involved in the work of ministry?

∾ When John says, "Do not imitate what is evil, but what is good," what is his specific context? In other words, what exactly is the situation he has in mind?

∾ How are you imitating what is good? What is evil?

THOUGHT FOR THE WEEK

Second John addresses the issue of deceivers or false teachers. These people were outside of the church. They may have been in the church at one time, but by the time John wrote they had "gone out into the world" (2 John 7). In 2 John two characteristics set them apart from believers. In relation to God, they denied the humanity of Jesus. In relation to others, they did not walk in love. In this letter, John the elder addresses a problem *within* the church.

Diotrephes and Gaius are both leaders in the church. However, their attitudes are radically different. Gaius is a man of hospitality, but Diotrephes is inhospitable. One loved to meet the needs of traveling Christians—in this case, men sent by John the elder. One loved to be the center of attention. Diotrephes refused to be hospitable and refused to allow others to help. His attitude is almost the same as the deceivers'—he did not walk in love.

Jesus was very clear that the attitude of believers is to be one of love. Anyone who acts in an unloving manner is to be suspect. Hospitality, or showing kindness to others, is not the exclusive attribute of Christians, but it is to be one of our dominant characteristics. Loving others by showing kindness is a good way to advertise God to the world, and it is good practice for learning humility.

Ask God to open your eyes to the needs of people around you and then meet those needs. Your action could be as simple as a warm smile, a word of encouragement, or even a random act of kindness.

Are you making a habit of being hospitable? Do you invite others into your home? If the answer is no, then start now. You might start small—have someone over for dessert after church. But please start.

Oh, and one last thing. Don't wait for others to be kind—show them how. Be hospitable.

Theme of 3 John:

SEGMENT DIVISIONS	PARAGRAPH THEMES	
		Author:
	VERSE 1	Date:
	VERSES 2-4	Purpose:
	VERSES 5-8	Key Words:
	VERSES 9-10	
	VERSES 11-12	
	VERSES 13-15	

$\mathcal{P}$HILEMON

LOVE
RECONCILES

The book we call Philemon is actually a personal letter. Usually letters in the New Testament were addressed to specific churches or to the church in general, but this is a personal letter from the apostle Paul to a friend. It may be one of the most unique documents in the Bible.

This letter is only 25 verses long and fewer than 500 words in English, yet it is a masterpiece of letter writing. This week you have the opportunity to take a peek into the personal life of one of the founding fathers of Christianity, the apostle Paul. We will look at relationships in his life and how he handled difficult problems in those relationships. We will see his heart, his faith, and his Christianity in action. And in the process we will also learn truth for our relationships.

DAY ONE

As with the other letters you have studied, we will start each day by reading through Philemon. Today read Philemon at least twice. Mark each reference to the author with a blue circle, and mark each mention of the recipient with a red box. (Although Apphia and Archippus are mentioned in the opening remarks, Philemon is the intended recipient of this letter.) Draw an orange line under *Onesimus.* Draw a black arch over the word *slave.*

When you have finished, list in your notebook what you learn about these three men, paying close attention to the relationship they have. How would you describe that relationship?

In this letter, Paul describes himself as a prisoner of Jesus Christ and refers to his imprisonment several times. Most scholars believe Paul was in prison at Rome during the time of this writing.

DAY TWO

Today we will look at some background information you may find helpful in understanding this book. Start your study time by reading Philemon.

Paul wrote another letter in which he mentioned some of the same people you have been reading about. The book of Colossians is Paul's letter to the church in the city of Colossae. Colossae, Hierapolis, and Laodicea were three cities located close together in a valley about 100 miles east of Ephesus. These cities shared a lot of commerce and a great Roman road system.

Colossians 4:7-18 contains Paul's closing remarks to that church. In these remarks you will find some familiar names. Working through these verses may seem a little daunting because the names are strange and hard to pronounce. Relax—you don't have to know how to pronounce the names. There will not be a test. Besides, the first-century believers would have a little trouble pronouncing our names also.

Read Colossians 4:7-18 and mark each reference to *Onesimus* just as you did in Philemon. Add any new information to your list on Onesimus in your notebook. Also, underline any reference to *Archippus* (see Philemon 2).

Since Paul was a prisoner, he could not have delivered this letter to Colossae. So, according to 4:7-9, who are the letter carriers?

DAY THREE

As you have seen, the letter to Colossae and the letter to Philemon were probably penned at the same time and delivered by Tychicus and Onesimus.

Read through Philemon once again. This time, mark each reference to *love* with a heart just as you have been doing. Be sure to mark synonyms such as *heart* or *beloved*. Underline in red any phrase using the words *heart* and *refresh*.

Onesimus, a runaway slave, faced the possibility of the death penalty. According to Philemon 18, Onesimus may have even stolen goods or money from his master.

His situation with Philemon was serious. He needed someone to intercede on his behalf. He needed someone to reconcile him to Philemon. In similar fashion, we have sinned against God. Read the following passages and note what you learn about why we can have a relationship with God and our hope for reconciliation.

- Romans 5:6-10
- Titus 2:14

DAY FOUR

Are you falling in love with this letter yet? Every reading of it seems to produce a new appreciation for the beauty and depth of this book, doesn't it?

Well, today we want you to start your time in the Word just as you have been doing—by reading Philemon. You do not need to mark anything this time. When you have finished, read the following passages and note what you learn about Jesus.

- ∾ 1 Timothy 2:5-6
- ∾ Hebrews 7:23-25

Paul interceded with Philemon on behalf of Onesimus. In a similar fashion, we need someone to intercede on our behalf. As members of the human race we have all sinned against God. We desperately need an intercessor. Jesus himself pleads our case; Jesus intercedes on your behalf before the Father! What an awesome truth!

DAY FIVE

Friend, can you identify with Philemon? Has someone you trusted hurt you? Abandoned you? Unfortunately, relationships often involve pain. The pain of rejection, the pain of abandonment, and the pain of a confidence broken are all too common in relationships. As a Christian, how are you supposed to handle the offense? What do you do?

The Bible has answers. You have already seen what Paul expected from Philemon. What does Jesus expect from us?

Read Matthew 18:21-35. As you read, mark *forgive* with a red box and shade it blue. Mark *repay* with a green box. Note what you learn about forgiveness.

DAY SIX

Perhaps you can identify with Onesimus because you have run from something you know you should have stayed with. Maybe you have injured someone or stolen something. If you are the guilty party, how do you handle it? What do you do?

Before we look at any cross-references, reread Philemon. As you read, ask yourself what Paul expected of Onesimus. From what you saw in Colossians 4, who delivered the letter to Philemon?

Now, read the following verses and note the action you are to take if you are the guilty party.

- ∾ Numbers 5:5-8
- ∾ Matthew 5:23-24
- ∾ 1 John 1:8-10

One last thing for today. Complete your AT A GLANCE chart on page 80.

DAY SEVEN

 Store in your heart: Philemon 7
Read and discuss: Philemon

QUESTIONS FOR DISCUSSION OR INDIVIDUAL STUDY

∾ What did you learn this week about Paul?

∾ What was the relationship between Onesimus and Philemon?

∾ How does this relationship change? Why?

∾ Why do you believe Paul chose to make a request of Philemon rather than order him?

∾ What relationship principles does Paul model?

∾ What implications of the gospel do you see applied in this letter?

∾ Who do you most identify with in this letter? Why?

∾ What did you learn about forgiveness this week?

∾ What have you learned about confession of sin?

∾ How is reconciliation played out in this letter? In the gospel of Jesus Christ?

THOUGHT FOR THE WEEK

This letter is an incredible example of the principles of reconciliation. First, two people were in need of reconciliation, and Paul sought a way to accomplish it. We needed to be reconciled to God, and Jesus found a way to accomplish it.

Second, Paul interceded on behalf of Onesimus. In a very real sense he took the side of the guilty in calling for forgiveness. Jesus pleads our case before the Father—He intercedes on our behalf.

Third, concerning the debt that Onesimus owed Philemon, Paul said, "Charge that to my account." Jesus took our debt to God and paid it.

Fourth, Paul initiated the reconciliation. He brought Philemon and Onesimus together; through Paul, reconciliation occurred. In Christ, humanity and Deity are reconciled. We were estranged from God, guilty, and deserving the death penalty. Jesus accepted the penalty on our behalf and paid it in full. John records Jesus' last words on the cross in John 19:30. Jesus said, "It is finished." This phrase translates one Greek word, *tetelestai*, which emphasizes the completeness of an action. It was a very common Greek word that indicated that the payment of a debt had been made in full. In other words, Jesus paid your debt in full on the cross with His death.

This letter gives us incredible insight into the heart and faith of the apostle. He demonstrated the implications of the gospel. He lived out what he preached.

Are you living out the implications of the gospel?

PHILEMON AT A GLANCE

Theme of Philemon:

	SEGMENT DIVISIONS	PARAGRAPH THEMES
Author:		
Date:		VERSES 1-3
Purpose:		VERSES 4-7
Key Words:		VERSES 8-16
		VERSES 17-20
		VERSES 21-22
		VERSES 23-25

JAMES

INTRODUCTION TO JAMES

James was the half brother of Jesus. During Jesus' earthly ministry, James didn't believe his older brother was the Messiah, the promised One from God (John 7:3-5). He was probably among the family members who thought Jesus had lost His mind and tried to take Him into custody (Mark 3:21,31). James was apparently convinced by Jesus' appearance to him after His resurrection from the dead (1 Corinthians 15:7). From that point on James was a dedicated follower of our Lord. He went on to became a leader in the church in Jerusalem. Later, when local persecution had driven many Christians out of Jerusalem, James wrote a letter to the believers who were scattered throughout the Roman world.

So for the next five weeks, we will study this short letter and learn everything we can about the Christian life. Along the way you will learn about relationships—how to love one another and even how to love our enemies.

THE PURPOSE OF TRIALS

Trials? We all have to face them! Many times they come in the form of relationships. What do you need to know to survive? How can you handle them? Can any good come from a trial? This first chapter of James has practical answers.

DAY ONE

Always begin your study time with prayer. The Bible is God's book, so ask Him to open your understanding and reveal *His* truth to you.

James structures his writing distinctively. Once you see the pattern he uses, you will better understand the flow of the book. First, he introduces a subject with a statement or an instruction. For example, in James 1:2 he introduces the subject of trials by saying, "Consider it all joy, my brethren, when you encounter various trials." James then follows with more instructions, illustrations, or explanations of the subject he has introduced.

Your first assignment is to read James 1. Read slowly, taking your time. As you read, mark the recipients of the letter (usually *you* or *your*) with a red box.

As you have seen, we generally use the color red for the recipients, but you are free to develop your own marking system.

If you have not already done so, please read "How to Get Started" at the beginning of this book. The information there is designed to help you succeed in Bible study and to keep you from becoming frustrated.

After you have read James 1, think through these questions:

~ What are the major subjects covered?

~ How are these subjects relevant to my life?

DAY TWO

"Consider it all joy...when you encounter various trials" (James 1:2). You may be skeptical of this advice. Can anyone consider it all joy when they are in the middle of a trial? Well, before we answer that question, let's look at the whole passage and see what James tells us about trials.

Read James 1:1-11 and mark each reference to *faith* like this: /faith/ and shade it green. Mark *God* with a triangle and *Jesus* with a cross as you have before.

After you read verses 1-11 and mark the words, list in your notebook what James teaches concerning trials. Be sure to note the instructions he gives concerning dealing with trials.

As we study this book together, write the subject James is discussing in the margin of your Bible. This will enable you to see at a glance what subjects he covers. For example, next to James 1:2 you can write *trials* in the margin.

DAY THREE

This is going to sound redundant, but read James 1:1-11 again today. The constant reading and rereading of passages plants them in your mind. As you go over them you will begin to see a depth in the Word you would not see otherwise. Therefore, taking your time, read James 1:1-11.

Now, let's cross-reference James' teaching with Paul's in Romans 5:1-5. Read this passage and mark every reference to *God* and *Jesus Christ.*

From Romans 5:3-5, list in your notebook some of the things that happen as the result of trials. This assignment is essential for a right understanding of trials, so take your time and don't miss anything.

DAY FOUR

James has a positive attitude about trials; most of the rest of us, however, do not. Still, we have to deal with them, so let's continue the study and learn everything we can about how to handle trials. As we begin today, put yourself back into context by reading James 1:1-11. Then read 1 Peter 1:3-9 and mark each reference to *God* and *Jesus Christ.*

When you have finished, record in your notebook the additional insights you gain concerning trials.

DAY FIVE

Start by reading James 1:1-11. If you are tempted to skip this part, then reread the comments from day 3.

James said we are to count it all joy when we encounter various trials. The word "various" is a translation of the Greek word *poikilos*. Peter used this word twice in his first letter—you saw "various trials" yesterday in 1 Peter 1:6. Today we will look at the second occurrence in 1 Peter. Read 1 Peter 4:10-19. As you read, underline the word *manifold,* and mark each reference to *suffering* (including any synonyms) like this: suffering.

List in your notebook what you learned about dealing with trials. Interesting, isn't it? You face multifaceted trials as a steward of the multifaceted grace of God.

DAY SIX

This is the last assignment for this week. If you faithfully completed your assignments this week you learned a lot about trials. Accurately understanding the teachings of God's Word about trials is beneficial for two reasons. First, and most obviously, it helps you respond properly to trials. We all face them. Knowing why they occur and how to walk through them makes it easier. Second, we are able to comfort, encourage, and instruct others.

Today let's look at one more passage dealing with trials. Turn in your Bible to 2 Corinthians 1:1-12. Read this passage and mark *affliction* (and any synonyms) in red just as you marked *suffering* yesterday. Shade the word *comfort* (and any synonyms) in blue.

List in your notebook all this passage teaches you about trials and comfort.

How do these teachings relate to those in 1 Peter 4:10 and James 1:2?

DAY SEVEN

Store in your heart: James 1:5

Read and discuss: James 1:1-11.

QUESTIONS FOR DISCUSSION OR INDIVIDUAL STUDY

∾ Discuss what you learned from James 1 about trials.

∾ What is the result of the testing of your faith?

∾ What additional insights did you gain from your study of 1 Peter 1 and 1 Peter 4?

∾ According to Romans 5, what are some of the benefits of trials?

∾ What else do you learn about facing trials from Romans 5?

∾ According to 2 Corinthians 1, how and why are we comforted in trials?

∾ How does this compare with what you learned in 1 Peter 4:10?

∾ After all you have learned this week, how can you come alongside someone who is going through a trial and help them?

∾ What are some of the possible outcomes of trials?

∾ Who determines the outcomes of trials?

∾ List some practical steps you can take this week as you face trials.

THOUGHT FOR THE WEEK

Trials. We all go through them. They are a part of every-one's life and very often involve relationships. Difficult people step into our lives, and we suddenly find ourselves in a trial. They are common, so why are we surprised when we encounter them? One of the reasons is that trials are unex-pected. You're walking along, minding your own business, and suddenly without warning you're in a trial.

So how do we prepare for trials? First, by knowing they're coming. God's Word says you *will* be tried—your faith *will* be tested. James says trials will be sudden or without warning, meaning you will stumble into them unexpectedly. But that doesn't mean you can't be ready. You may not know *when* they are coming, but you do know they are coming.

Second, we can focus on the value of the trial in the life of the believer. Trials produce strength and endurance. They purify faith and cause us to mature.

Third, we can ask for wisdom. God will grant it. He will not leave us alone without guidance.

Finally, keep entrusting yourself to God Most High. He will see that the fire is never too hot for you to handle (1 Corinthians 10:13). Growing through trials is a great way to show the world we are different from unbelievers. We don't have to be defeated—we can live in victory.

THE SOURCE
OF TEMPTATION

Temptations. We all face them. Sometimes we walk in victory, and then sometimes we fail. What are temptations? Where do they come from? What can you do to improve your ability to resist? This week we will find the answers in God's Word.

DAY ONE

James uses essentially the same Greek word for *trials* and *temptations*. Generally he uses the noun form for *trial* and the verb form for *temptation*. The root Greek word is *peira*, which basically means to test, or to experience testing. Trials come upon us from the outside—we stumble into or encounter them. What about temptation? Is the source outside us as it is with trials or from within?

Today read James 1:12-18. Mark each reference to *God* and *Jesus* (including pronouns). Color the word *sin* brown.

As you did before with trials, list in your notebook what you learn about temptations. Include any instructions James gives for handling them. Be sure to catch the progression in verses 14-15. It is important that you see the result of temptation when it is not handled well.

You may want to write *temptations* in the margin of your Bible next to 1:12.

DAY TWO

The Greek phrase *exelkómenos kaí deleazómenos* in James 1:14 is translated by the very descriptive phrase "carried away and enticed." It is a hunting or fishing metaphor. The word *exelkómenos* means to lure something out into the open. The word *deleazómenos* means bait. It is the idea of being lured into a snare by a bait. But where does the bait come from? Why is it tempting? Who is luring you away—someone else or your own heart?

Start today by reading James 1:12-18 to put yourself in context. Then read Proverbs 6:20-29. As you read, mark the word *heart* with a red heart but don't shade it as you have shaded *love*. Ask yourself why this temptation is so strong. Add any insights on temptation to your information in your notebook.

DAY THREE

We have highlighted one source of temptation. Now, how do I respond to temptation? Is there a way of escape? Friend, the Word has the answer. Read James 1:19-25.

Mark each reference to *God* and *word*. Mark *law* like this: law.

In your notebook, answer the Who? What? and Why? of this passage. Remember, this is not an isolated passage; it comes right after the discussion of trials and temptations. What does this teach you about dealing with trials and temptations?

DAY FOUR

Today we will continue to look at temptations and how you can have victory over them. Read the following verses, and in your notebook, write out what they teach you about temptation.

- ∞ 1 Corinthians 6:12-20
- ∞ 1 Corinthians 10:13
- ∞ Hebrews 4:15-16

DAY FIVE

How do you grow through trials and survive temptation? You have seen part of the answer, but let's look a little deeper at one aspect of James' answer. To put yourself in context read James 1:19-25. Now read the following verses and note what you learn about how the Word of God can help you in trials and temptations.

- ∞ Psalm 119:9-11
- ∞ Psalm 119:50
- ∞ Psalm 119:97-105
- ∞ Psalm 119:129-136

DAY SIX

You have seen the benefits of knowing and memorizing the Word. Today we will look at a key passage for the fight against temptation. You have seen that Satan tempted Jesus. He will tempt you also. You are in a war. How can you survive and fight effectively?

Read Ephesians 6:10-18. In your Bible, mark the phrase *stand firm*. You might want to shade it a particular color so you will be able to see it easily. Also, note each instruction or command. We suggest you use a red arrow in the margin of your Bible to point to each instruction.

List in your notebook each piece of armor along with the descriptions Paul (the author of Ephesians) includes.

DAY SEVEN

 Store in your heart: James 1:19-20
Read and discuss: James 1:12-25

QUESTIONS FOR DISCUSSION OR INDIVIDUAL STUDY

- ∾ What did you learn this week about temptations?

- ∾ Where do temptations come from?

- ∾ What tempts you?

- ∾ What are the possible outcomes of temptation? Who determines the outcome of temptation?

- ∾ How are you to respond to temptation?

∾ What did you learn about temptation and the Word?

∾ What does Psalm 119 teach you about the Word?

∾ How will knowing the Word make a difference in your fight against temptations?

∾ Discuss the armor of God and the usefulness of each piece.

THOUGHT FOR THE WEEK

Trials originate outside us, and they are designed to strengthen and mature us. Temptations originate within, and they can destroy us. James uses fishing language to describe temptation. The enemy of your soul is a master at designing just the right bait to lure you away from your devotion to the Lord. Satan designs the bait, but we are carried away by our own lusts. There is a real danger in always blaming the enemy for our temptations when actually the source is our own lusts. Satan masterfully designs the lure, but the motivation to bite comes from our own lusts. Beware, my friend. The tempting morsel has a hook. Jesus said in John 8:34, "Truly, truly, I say to you, everyone who commits sin is the slave of sin." You see, once that hook is set in you the enemy has a measure of control over you, and he will try to destroy you. Beware! Satan hates you and has a horrible plan for your life.

How do you defend yourself against temptation? First, pray! In Matthew 6:7-13 Jesus is teaching His disciples a prayer they can use as a model. In verse 13 He says to pray, "And do not lead us into temptation, but deliver us from evil." Prayer is vital to withstanding temptation. Pray that you will not be tempted. When you are tempted, pray for direction.

Second, put on the whole armor of God, as you were told to do in Ephesians 6. Each piece of the armor is centered in the Word of God. The more you become familiar with the Word, the stronger you will be.

In addition to studying, memorizing Scripture is a very effective tool. You can start by memorizing passages that relate to specific temptations you have. For example, men should find it helpful to memorize Matthew 5:27-28: "You have heard that it was said, 'You shall not commit adultery'; but I say to you that everyone who looks at a woman with lust for her has already committed adultery with her in his heart."

Any of us—male or female—would benefit from memorizing 1 Corinthians 6:19-20, which you studied this week. In addition to memorizing a specific verse to address a specific problem, you would do well to commit Romans 6 to memory. When you become conscious of thoughts you know you should not have, thoughts you don't want anyone else to know about, start quoting Romans 6. The enemy gets tired of hearing you quote Scripture and will drop the fight—at least for the moment.

Following these tactics will give you victory over temptation. When people around you see you walking in victory they will want what you have—a relationship with Jesus Christ.

LOVE YOUR NEIGHBOR

There's a line from an old gospel song that says, "Faith without works is like a song you can't sing. It's just about as worthless as a screen door on a submarine." Faith without works—James has a lot to say about this subject. This week we will explore what James teaches concerning the relationship of faith and works.

DAY ONE

Last week we finished studying James 1, except for two little verses at the end. Today your time will be spent taking a closer look at these two verses. Read verses 26 and 27 and mark *religion* or *religious* with a capital R. Draw a small heart over the word *heart*. Draw a small wavy line through the word *tongue*.

(By the way, you will be marking the word *tongue* again in chapter 3.) After you finish reading and marking, list in your notebook exactly how James defines *religion*. Be sure to include both verses in your definition.

Record the theme of James 1 on the JAMES AT A GLANCE chart on page 113. What two subjects does James discuss in chapter 1?

DAY TWO

Today read James 2 and mark each reference to *God* and *Jesus Christ* just as you did in chapter one. Be sure to include pronouns. When you have finished, read James 2 a second time and mark each reference to the recipients of the letter. Reading it twice and while slowing down to mark key words and phrases will help you see the flow of thought. Don't short-circuit the learning process by just reading it once. Remember, friend, your goal is to know God and His Word, not simply to finish each assignment.

DAY THREE

How do you treat other people? Do you ever treat some people better than others because they have a position of influence or because they are wealthy? Don't answer too quickly—we've probably all done this. Is this okay? Is it wrong? Does the Word of God offer any guidance?

As you studied James 1 you saw how James introduces a subject with a statement or an instruction and then discusses it. Read James 2:1 and identify the major subject James is about to discuss.

Now read James 2:1-13 and mark every reference to the word *law* like this: law. When you have finished, list in your notebook everything you learn about treating others with favoritism.

As you did in James 1, you might want to write the theme of James 2:1-13 in the margin of your Bible next to verse 1 so you can see quickly and easily the subjects James deals with.

DAY FOUR

Faith and works. Are they mutually exclusive terms, or do they complement each other? Let's see what the Word of God says.

Read James 2:14-26 and mark every reference to *faith* the same way you did in chapter 1. Mark *works* with a bold **W**.

When you have finished, start a new topic in your notebook: "Faith and Works." List in your notebook everything you learn about them.

DAY FIVE

James uses events in Abraham's life to show the relationship between faith and works. Today you will look a little closer at this example from the Old Testament. Start by reading James 2:14-26 to put yourself back into context. Since James 2:23 quotes Genesis 15:6, read Genesis 15:1-6 to learn everything you can about Abraham's faith. In your notebook answer the following questions:

- ∾ What did Abraham do to be reckoned righteous before God?
- ∾ Was this before or after the birth of Isaac?
- ∾ Which came first—Abraham's faith or the offering of Isaac?

DAY SIX

You have seen that the best commentary on Scripture is Scripture. You have already done some cross-referencing in this study, and today we will have you do a little more. Read Ephesians 2:8-10. As you read, be sure to note how we are saved and what we are created for. Which comes first— faith or works? Now, answer the same question from James 2:14-26. Again, which comes first, faith or works?

Don't forget to add the theme of James 2 on JAMES AT A GLANCE.

DAY SEVEN

 Store in your heart: James 2:12-13
Read and discuss: James 1:26-27; 2:1-26; and the cross-references

QUESTIONS FOR DISCUSSION OR INDIVIDUAL STUDY

- What are the major subjects James discusses in chapter 2?
- According to James, what is pure and undefiled religion?
- How should this definition affect the way you "do church"?
- What steps do you need to take to make sure your personal "religion" is pure and undefiled?
- What did you learn this week about showing favoritism?
- What are some of the ways favoritism is expressed in our culture? In our churches?
- What did you learn this week about faith and works?

∾ What is the relationship between faith and works?

∾ In what ways will your faith be expressed by what you do?

∾ How does James expect you to express your faith by your works?

∾ What have you learned this week about relating to others?

∾ Do people who know you see Christ expressed in your walk?

Thought for the Week

What is the relationship between works and faith? What is the relationship between what you believe and what you do? James 2:14 says, "What use is it, my brethren, if someone says he has faith but he has no works? Can that faith save him?" In the Greek, the words translated "says" and "has" are present tense, representing the idea of continuous action. In other words, the person is always saying he has faith, but he never has the works to prove it. That person, in James' estimation, has a worthless faith—a faith that can't save. In James 2:22 he adds that faith is perfected by works. The Greek word translated "perfected" means to bring something to completeness or to bring it to its goal. The goal or completeness of faith is expressed in the works it produces.

In Matthew 7:16 Jesus says we can identify false teachers by their fruit. He goes on to say that grapes are not gathered from thorn bushes and figs do not come from thistles. His point is that a tree can be identified by its fruit. We can all be identified as followers of Christ or not by the things we do. Our works occur because we are followers of Christ, not the other way around. Saving faith produces evident behavioral patterns. Those behaviors are seen very often in the way we treat others.

What kind of fruit are you producing? Look to your relationships with others to find out.

WATCH
YOUR MOUTH

"Sticks and stones may break my bones, but words will never hurt me." It was a catchy phrase when you were eight. However, you knew even back then that it was not true. Actually, some of the things we say hurt a lot more than physical pain. And the scars take longer to heal. Words can hurt, but they can also heal, encourage, and strengthen. It is all in the power of the tongue. Relationships are built up or destroyed by what we say. How do you use your tongue? How are you supposed to? Let's see what God has to say.

This week, as you work through the assignments, ask God to reveal to you the effect of your words on other people, especially your family. Ask Him to show you your strengths and how to improve your weaknesses in the area of communication.

DAY ONE

Today read James 3 and mark each reference to the recipients of the letter, just as you have been doing. Also, mark each reference to *God*. Then read James 3 a second time and draw a small wavy line through each reference to the *tongue*. Draw a cloud around each reference to *wisdom* and shade it yellow.

When you have finished, write in the margin of your Bible the main topics James addresses in chapter 3. List in your notebook what James tells you about the tongue.

DAY TWO

The tongue is obviously very powerful and very hard to control. Why is the tongue hard to control? Read the following passages and mark each reference to the *mouth* or to speaking just as you marked *tongue*. Mark *heart* with a small heart. Note what you learn about the relationship between the mouth and the heart.

- ∾ Matthew 12:33-37
- ∾ Matthew 15:18-20

DAY THREE

Read James 2:14-26 to put yourself back into context. Now let's get to the heart of the matter (pun intended). Read the following passages and note what you learn. In your notebook answer this question: How can we control our tongue?

- ∾ Ezekiel 36:26-27
- ∾ John 7:37-39

DAY FOUR

So far this week you have seen from Scripture that the tongue is hard to control and why. You have also seen God's answer for controlling the tongue—a new heart. Now before we move on to another subject, let's look at how the tongue is supposed to act. Read the following passages and note in your notebook what you learn:

- ∾ Proverbs 16:21-24
- ∾ Proverbs 18:21
- ∾ Ephesians 4:29
- ∾ Colossians 4:6

DAY FIVE

It's interesting that James discusses the tongue first and then wisdom because sometimes the tongue says things that seem so unwise. Today we will look at the rest of James 3 to learn what we can about wisdom. Your assignment is to read James 3:13-18. When you have finished, list in your notebook what you learn about wisdom. Make a two-column chart. In one column, list what the text says about wisdom from above; in the other, list what you learn about earthly wisdom.

Don't forget to fill in your JAMES AT A GLANCE chart for chapter 3.

DAY SIX

Your final assignment this week is to read James 4 twice. The first time, mark each reference to *God* and *Jesus*. The second time, mark the recipients with a red box. Draw a pitchfork through the word *demonic*. Mark *sin* by shading it brown.

When you finish, record in the margin of your Bible the major subjects James covers in chapter 4. You don't need to get too detailed; we just want you to see the big picture.

DAY SEVEN

Store in your heart: James 3:2

Read and discuss: James 3 and the cross-references

QUESTIONS FOR DISCUSSION OR INDIVIDUAL STUDY

∽ What did you learn this week about the tongue?

∽ Discuss the two illustrations James uses to show the power of the tongue.

∽ Give examples (good and bad) from your life that demonstrate the power of the tongue.

∽ How should believers communicate?

∽ What is the relationship between the heart and the tongue?

∽ How can you control your tongue? Discuss the cross-references you looked at this week.

∽ What are some practical ways you can speak to your family members or friends to encourage them this week?

∽ What is the relationship between wisdom and the tongue?

∾ What are the differences between earthly and godly wisdom?

∾ Judging by your speech, your attitudes, and your actions, which kind of wisdom do you have?

THOUGHT FOR THE WEEK

A children's song says,

> Be careful little tongue what you say,
> be careful little tongue what you say.
> For the Father up above is looking down in love,
> be careful little tongue what you say.

We learn so much truth as children, and yet we carry little of it into adulthood. How much grief we would save others and ourselves if we remembered those lessons and were careful with what we said. Carefully chosen words can change the course of a child's life, disarm the accuser, calm the storm, build up the depressed, and give hope to the hopeless. Just think what would happen if we always chose our words carefully before we spoke.

Positive, encouraging communication is very powerful. You shape and form people and situations with your words. When you show gentleness and love in your conversations with family and friends, you demonstrate that they are important and that they are loved. The result is that your conversation helps to protect them in a cruel and harsh world. Just by offering gentle conversation you can be a refuge to them. How pleased would God be if everyone He placed in your life thought of you as a safe and warm refuge simply because of the way you communicated with them? Jesus said the two greatest commandments are to love God and to love others (Mark 12:29-31). Expressing our love to God includes using our voices in singing, worship, and prayer. Expressing love to people also involves using our voices. Our communication should build up, strengthen, and encourage, not put down and criticize.

Ask God to show you how you are doing. Are you encouraging those around you, or are you more often complaining and criticizing?

DRAW NEAR
TO GOD

A pastor once remarked while teaching on humility that perhaps the listeners should read his book on the subject, *Humility and How I Achieved It,* along with the companion book, *The Ten Most Humble Men in America and How I Chose the Other Nine.* Of course he was only kidding.

This week you will see some of the outward signs of pride—the opposite of humility—and how pride injures relationships. James will also give you the cure. Our prayer is that the Holy Spirit will show you how this character quality is developing in your life.

DAY ONE

Today read the first ten verses of James 4. In your notebook, list the reasons for quarrels and unanswered prayers. If you could sum up all of the reasons into one phrase, what would it be?

When James addresses a problem, he also gives a solution. Read 4:1-10 again and this time list in your notebook the imperatives James gives in these verses. An imperative is a command or instruction. For example, in 4:7 the first imperative is "Submit therefore to God." If the problem is found in verses 1-5, what is the solution in verses 6-10?

DAY TWO

Friendship with the world is hostility toward God. Have you ever thought about life that way? Being friends with one means being an enemy of the other. But James uses an even stronger term—"adulteresses." Why does James use this term? Were the only guilty ones women? Of course not. To understand James' use of the term *adulteresses* look up the following verses and note who is married to whom. What does this teach you about your relationship to God?

   ∽ Jeremiah 31:31-32

   ∽ Revelation 19:6-8 (*The Lamb* is a reference to Jesus.)

DAY THREE

Do you ever find yourself making plans but leaving God out? James has a warning for you, friend. Read James 4:13-17. Note exactly what James' readers have been boasting about. Is planning for the future wrong? What exactly is the sin James is addressing? To get another perspective, read Luke 12:16-21. Spend the rest of your time today in prayer, asking God to show you areas of your life where you are guilty of arrogance by not planning everything around Him.

Be sure to list the major subjects of James 4 on your JAMES AT A GLANCE chart.

DAY FOUR

Today we begin our study of the last chapter of the book of James. James has a few more things to say to us about life.

Today read James chapter 5. As you read, mark each reference to *Lord*, including synonyms.

Read James 5 a second time and mark each reference to the recipients with a red box.

In the margin of your Bible, note the major subjects James addresses in chapter 5. Of course, you may be tempted to read the chapter only once, marking everything at once. Don't—you will only be cheating yourself. Read it twice.

DAY FIVE

What is your attitude toward money? How generous are you? What should your attitude toward money be? Today read James 5:1-6. In your notebook, answer the following questions.

- ∾ What eventually happens to material wealth?
- ∾ Why?
- ∾ What are the rich doing?
- ∾ What are they not doing?

When you have finished, read James 5:7-11. As you read, underline the words *patient* and *patience*. If you are suffering because of mistreatment at the hands of some rich person, what is your response to be?

DAY SIX

This is your last assignment in James. We realize this has been a fast five weeks and many of the subjects in James were not covered in depth. We have a Precept Upon Precept study in James that is much deeper if you are interested. It requires about an hour of homework a day, five days a week. The 15-week course gives you a solid grip on the teachings in this incredible little letter. For more information, contact Precept Ministries International www.precept.org, call 800-763-8280, or fill out and mail the response card at the back of the book.

Today, read James 5:13-20. As you read, mark any reference to *prayer* with an upward arrow.

List in your notebook the process for dealing with someone who is physically ill.

We don't have time in this study to fully cover this subject. However, the following passages will give you some insight into Elijah's prayer.

- ∽ 1 Kings 16:29–17:7 (This is the beginning of the story of Elijah. Note what the king has done to provoke the Lord.)

- ∽ Deuteronomy 11:8-17 (Moses is speaking. The children of Israel are about to move into the promised land under the leadership of Joshua.)

Where do you think Elijah got the idea to say what he did? Was Elijah operating independently of the Lord? What does this teach you about prayer specifically in relation to James 5?

Record the theme of James 5 on the JAMES AT A GLANCE chart and add the theme of the entire book.

DAY SEVEN

Store in your heart: James 5:7-8

Read and discuss: James 4–5 and cross-references

QUESTIONS FOR DISCUSSION OR INDIVIDUAL STUDY

∞ According to James 4, what caused the problems the people were having?

∞ In what ways do we see the same problems among believers today?

∞ What does the word "adulteress" in James 4:4 imply?

∞ In what ways do we show our unfaithfulness to God today?

∞ Do you always consider God in your plans?

∞ Give examples of times you made plans without considering God and things went wrong.

∞ What is the attitude we should have toward money? Why?

∞ What did you learn this week about God holding people accountable for the way they treat others?

∞ What did you learn this week about prayer? How will this affect your prayer life?

∞ What is the sick person's responsibility?

∞ Discuss the most significant truth God has shown you personally in your study of James.

THOUGHT FOR THE WEEK

Is God's will the first thing you think of when you are making plans? If you are a Christian you will probably answer yes. You probably would consider what the will of God is when making big decisions. Life-changing decisions like marriage, college, and careers are ones we all pray about. But do His desires cross your mind in the day-to-day decisions of life?

James 4 condemns the businessman because he did not consider God in making a simple business plan. The plan to do business in a certain city was probably logical. The local economy may have been good, the local taxes favorable, the local chamber of commerce helpful. On paper it was undoubtedly a great business plan. The one problem was he had not considered what God's plan might be. That is arrogance.

An outward sign of arrogance can reveal more than simply a haughty attitude. Proud people make their plans and leave God out.

Have you asked God what He has in mind for the simple things in life? Have you asked God about the clothing you wear or the food you eat? Have you asked Him if you are going to have lunch today or fast? Start your day with prayer and seek God's will for the little things—even the daily decisions.

Theme of James:

SEGMENT
DIVISIONS

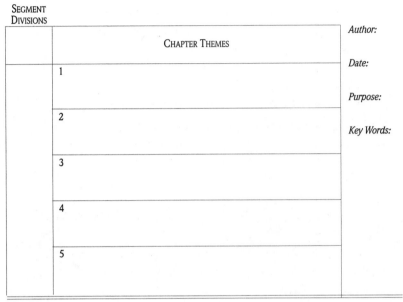

CHAPTER THEMES

1

2

3

4

5

Author:

Date:

Purpose:

Key Words:

Notes for Personal Study

NOTES FOR PERSONAL STUDY

NOTES FOR PERSONAL STUDY

NOTES FOR PERSONAL STUDY

NOTES FOR PERSONAL STUDY

Notes for Personal Study

BOOKS IN THE
NEW INDUCTIVE STUDY SERIES

❧❧❧❧

Teach Me Your Ways
Genesis, Exodus,
Leviticus, Numbers,
Deuteronomy

*Choosing Victory,
Overcoming Defeat*
Joshua, Judges, Ruth

Desiring God's Own Heart
1 & 2 Samuel,
1 Chronicles

Walking Faithfully with God
1 & 2 Kings, 2 Chronicles

*Overcoming Fear
and Discouragement*
Ezra, Nehemiah, Esther

*Trusting God
in Times of Adversity*
Job

*God's Blueprint for
Bible Prophecy*
Daniel

*Opening the Windows
of Blessings*
Haggai, Zechariah,
Malachi

The Call to Follow Jesus
Luke

*The Holy Spirit
Unleashed in You*
Acts

*God's Answers for
Relationships and Passions*
1 & 2 Corinthians

*Free from Bondage
God's Way*
Galatians, Ephesians

That I May Know Him
Philippians, Colossians

*Standing Firm in
These Last Days*
1 & 2 Thessalonians

*Walking in Power,
Love, and Discipline*
1 & 2 Timothy, Titus

*Living with Discernment
in the End Times*
1 & 2 Peter, Jude

God's Love Alive in You
1, 2, & 3 John,
Philemon, James

Behold, Jesus Is Coming!
Revelation

Everybody, Everywhere, Anytime, Anyplace, Any Age...
Can Discover the Truth for Themselves

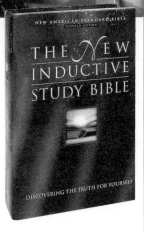

In today's world with its often confusing and mixed messages, where can you turn to find the answer to the challenges you and your family face? Whose word can you trust? Where can you turn when you need answers—about relationships, your children, your future?

The <u>Updated</u> New Inductive Study Bible

Open *this* study Bible and you will soon discover its uniqueness— unlike any other, this study Bible offers no notes, commentaries, or the opinions of others telling you what the Scripture is saying. It is in fact the only study Bible based entirely on the *inductive* study approach, providing you with instructions and the tools for observing what the text really says, interpreting what it means, and applying its principles to your life.

The only study Bible containing the *inductive study method* taught and endorsed by Kay Arthur and Precept Ministries.

• A new *smaller* size makes it easier to carry • individualized instructions for studying *every* book • guides for color marking keywords and themes • *Updated* NASB text • *improved* in-text maps and charts • 24 pages of full-color charts, historical timelines, & maps • self-discovery in its truest form

One Message, The Bible.
One Method, Inductive.

A SIMPLE, PROVEN APPROACH TO LETTING GOD'S WORD CHANGE YOUR LIFE...FOREVER

HARVEST HOUSE PUBLISHERS
EUGENE, OREGON 97402
www.harvesthousepublishers.com

Digging Deeper

∾∾∾∾

Books in the New Inductive Study Series are survey courses. If you want to do a more in-depth study of a particular book of the Bible, we suggest that you do a Precept Upon Precept Bible Study Course on that book. The Precept studies require approximately five hours of personal study a week. You may obtain more information on these powerful courses by contacting Precept Ministries International at 800-763-8280, visiting our website at www.precept.org, or filling out and mailing the response card in the back of this book.

If you desire to expand and sharpen your skills, you would really benefit by attending a Precept Ministries Institute of Training. The Institutes are conducted throughout the United States, Canada, and in a number of other countries. Class lengths vary from one to five days, depending on the course you are interested in. For more information about the Precept Ministries Institute of Training, call Precept Ministries.

YES, I WANT TO GROW SPIRITUALLY. TELL ME MORE ABOUT

PRECEPT MINISTRIES INTERNATIONAL

Name _____

Address _____

City _____

State _____ Postal Code _____

Country _____

Daytime phone ( ) _____

Email address _____

Fax ( ) _____

Evening phone ( ) _____

PLEASE SEND ME INFO ON:

❑ Learning how to study the Bible

❑ Bible study material

❑ Radio Programs

❑ TV Programs

❑ Israel Bible Study Tour

❑ Paul's Epistles Study Tour to Greece

❑ Men's Conferences

❑ Women's Conferences

❑ Teen Conferences

❑ Couples' Conferences

❑ Other_____

❑ I want to partner with Precept Ministries

ENCLOSED IS MY DONATION FOR $_____

P.O. Box 182218 • Chattanooga, TN 37422-7218
(800) 763-8280 • (423) 892-6814 • Radio/TV (800) 763-1990
Fax: (423) 894-2449 • www.precept.org • Email: info@precept.org